DRUGS AND THEIR EFFECT UPON THE MIND

By Shaykh Muhammad Baazmool

© Al Furqaan NJ Publishing, USA

All rights reserved. No part of this publication may be reproduced in any language, stored in any retrieval system or transmitted in any form or by any means, whether electronic, mechanic, photocopying, recording or otherwise, without express permission of the copyright owner.

ISBN: 978-1-4951-2138-8

First Edition: Rajab 1435 A.H. / June 2014 C.E.

Cover Design: Strictly Sunnah Design
E-mail: info@strictlysunnah.com

Translation by: Aboo Ruqayyah Raha ibn Donald Batts

Revision of Translation by: Ihsan ibn Gerald Gonsalves
Typesetting & Formatting by: Aboo Sulaymaan Muhammad 'Abdul-Azim ibn Joshua Baker

E-mail: maktabatulirshad@gmail.com

Publisher's Information:
Al Furqaan NJ Publishing

E-mail: alfurqaannj@gmail.com

TABLE OF CONTENTS

THE DEFINITION OF NARCOTICS 4

THE RULING OF DRUG ABUSE 8

PRESERVATION OF THE FIVE NECESSITIES 9

THE EFFECTS OF DRUGS 10

THE REASONS FOR TRAVERSING UPON THE PATH OF DRUGS 19

TREATMENT AND COMBATTING THE PROBLEM 20

CLOSING 24

APPENDIX ONE: THE DANGER OF DRUGS 25

APPENDIX TWO: DRUG MONEY FROM BEFORE ISLAAM 33

APPENDIX THREE: DRUG MONEY FROM AFTER ISLAAM ... 34

THE DEFINITION OF NARCOTICS

The Linguistic Definition:

المُخَدِّر Mukhaddir is derived from الْخِدْر (i.e., a covering.) It is said:

الْـمَـرْأَةُ خَـدَّرَهَـا أَهْـلُـهَـا

The woman's family covered her.

This means that they guarded her and protected her from being dishonored. From this, the noun المُخَدِّر is applied to all of that which covers the intellect and causes it to depart.

The Scientific Definition:

المُخَدِّر is a chemical substance which causes drowsiness and sleep or the loss of awareness coupled with the easing of pain. Perhaps it could lead to the formation of a habit and addiction.

The word المُخَدِّر is translated as narcotic; which is derived from الإغريقية narcosis; which means to intoxicate or to make intoxicated. Due to this, neither stimulants nor hallucinogens are considered narcotic in accordance with this definition, however, alcohol may be considered from narcotics.

The Legal Definition:

Narcotics is a combination of substances which cause addiction and poisons the nervous system; using, growing, and manufacturing it is dangerous except for objectives which the law dictates and it is not to be used except through someone providing him with a license for that. This includes opium and its derivatives, hashish, hallucinogens, cocaine, and stimulants. However, alcohol, sedatives, and sleeping pills do not fall under the category of narcotics in spite of their harms and their susceptibility to cause addiction.[1]

The Definition Given by the Health Organization:

The Health Organization use the term: Psychological substance instead of narcotics; because the latter includes substances and usages which are for research or others which are customary and not prohibited or dangerous. However, we use the term narcotics and intend by it the substances which cause dependence (addiction) and using them is prohibited except for medical purposes or research; or the abuse of the substances and drugs are subject to cause psychological effects.

Some narcotics are natural substances and some are manufactured. This includes sedatives and hallucinogens or that which is derived from natural plants, such as Hashish, opium, heroin, marijuana,[2] cocaine, or the substances, which are inhaled, such as acetone and gasoline.

The Definition of Addiction

The scientific term is: dependence; and it is of two types:

1.) Psychological dependence
2.) Physical dependence

---

[1] Taken from the website of the Center of Toxicology in Makkah: makatoxicology.com
[2] The term marijuana is used in the west or Al-Baanjoo البانجو in some of the Arab lands, to describe Hashish or the narcotic that is derived from the leaves on the plant known as Cannabis Sativa and that which has been grown within the tropical regions and the temperate regions. Marijuana is the dried leaves and buds of the Cannabis.

Psychological Dependence:

This is the personal tendency compelling the addicted person toward the affecting substances or narcotic drugs such that it leads to psychological conditions and at times physical, resulting from using the narcotic substance at a level which inclines the addict to increase the dosage of the abused substance. It is that which is defined as tolerance (level) or endurance (level). A compelling yearning controls the addict, driving him to strive to attain the desired psychological substance through any means, at any price, in any way and under any circumstance, from that which will bring it about by way of abnormal actions. This state is called: dependency, to distinguish it from addiction and habit "Which includes (i.e. dependency) falling under the effects of other substances not classified as prohibited or dangerous narcotics, such as alcohol."

There are other substances which some governments prohibit while others have not prohibited, such as Qat. In addition, there are the customary substances that are not dangerous but they cause addiction such as tobacco and to a lesser extent, coffee and tea.

The point is that it is the addiction which occurs as a result of drug to a lesser extent. Narcotics vary in terms of the level of their effect, danger, and method of use.[3]

---

[3] Refer to: Health Premises of the Royal Order: The Health Damage of Drugs / Prepared by Dr. Muhammad 'Alee Al-Baar [Ramadan 14-8 H./April 1988 C.E.] (Comprised within the Symposium of the Effects of the Royal Order of the Death Penalty for Drug Traffickers) –Kingdom of Saudi Arabia-General Council for the Supervision of the Youth in conjunction with the National Committee for Combatting Drugs and the General Committee for Combatting Drugs (pg. 71)

Physical Addiction (Withdrawal):

This is the state that the addict is in when he ceases using the narcotic. It is a combination of symptoms which come about as a result of the body's attempt to rid itself of the effects of the toxins of the narcotic; and it varies based upon the type of narcotic. These symptoms are the most severe as it relates to opium and its derivatives; more specifically heroin, since its time period lasts between two and four days and it can result, for some addicts, in death.

From the examples of the symptoms of withdrawal as it relates to addiction to amphetamines (steroids and stimulants) are: depression, fatigue, sleep disorders, and nightmares.

As it relates to withdrawal from alcohol, the symptoms take the form of severe tremors, nausea, vomiting, feeling irritable, malady, weakness, quickening of the heartbeat, sweating, and profuse sweating, in addition to feelings of depression, audio and visual hallucinations and false ideas. Perhaps the afflicted person may kill whoever is in front of him with whatever metal instrument available, because he believes that this person has enmity towards him.

Episodes of drug withdrawal of alcohol or barbiturates lead to death at a rate ranging between 25-30 percent when they are not treated. Drug withdrawal of heroin or morphine lead to death at a rate ranging between 5-10 percent if not treated.[4]

---

[4] Refer to: Drugs: The Scourge of the Modern Society; Selected Research Studies by Dr. Sa'eed Al-Haffaar, University of Qatar 1993; also: The problem of Drug Abuse amongst the Youth; Psychological Research by Doctor 'Alaa-ud-Deen Kafaafee University of Qatar 1993; also: Drugs and Society: An Exhaustive Study by Dr. Mustafaa Swaif; Aalam Al-Ma'rifah Series; January 1996 (pgs. 17-18); and Health Premises of the

THE RULING OF DRUG ABUSE

Using them is Haraam. The Messenger of Allaah (ﷺ) prohibited every intoxicant. The Messenger of Allaah (ﷺ) also prohibited every harm and reciprocal harm. Also because Khamr is that which intoxicates the mind and narcotics intoxicate the mind; therefore its ruling is the same ruling as Khamr.[5]

Royal Order: The Health Damage of Drugs; pg. 8. Also refer to Mawsoo'ah Maqaatil-Societal and Psychological Subjects: Addiction: Narcotics, Alcohol, and Smoking from a Psychological Perspective; by way of Al-Jazeerah website, 2001/ Drugs are the Scourge of the Era.

[5] Ibn 'Abbaas said: *"Khamr has been prohibited in itself; in small amounts and in large amounts. As has every intoxicating drink."* Reported by An-Nasaa'ee (2/332), At-Tahaawee (2/324), Ahmad (59/109), At-Tabaraanee (no. 10837), and Aboo Nu'aym within Al-Hilyah; and it has been graded Saheeh by Al-Albaanee

PRESERVATION OF THE FIVE NECESSITIES

The necessities within Al-Islaam the preservation of which is commanded are as follows:

- ❖ Blood
- ❖ Intellect
- ❖ Honor
- ❖ Wealth
- ❖ Religion

Drugs conflict with the preservation of these five necessities, therefore their ruling is the same as the ruling of Khamr. Khamr is the mother of (all) vile evils. For it spoils the religion, the intellect, the person, the honor, and the wealth.

THE EFFECTS OF DRUGS

Narcotics have an effect upon the user by way of harms in his body, his soul, his intellect, his manners, and his connection with the environment around him. His religion, intellect, person, honor, and wealth are (all) spoiled (as a result); and these effects vary from one substance to the next and they vary in their level of danger. However, it is possible to make a general mention of them in that which follows:

- ❖ Sluggishness and laziness
- ❖ Loss of responsibility and recklessness
- ❖ Cognitive disorder and the causing of traffic accidents and accidents in the workplace
- ❖ They cause the addict to be susceptible to psychological, physical, and mental illnesses. Perhaps he can be afflicted with HIV (A.I.D.S.) if he uses contaminated or used needles.
- ❖ Anxiety and paranoia.

Some narcotics, such as meth or crack, can lead to severe changes to the brain.

Similarly, drugs can lead to a series of harms on an individual level; such as:

- ❖ The breaking up of families
- ❖ Ruining of the familial and societal ties
- ❖ Incapability in fulfillment of basic requirements for the individual and the family

In most cases, the addict—under the influence of the demand for the drugs—falls into a number of crimes; from them:

- ❖ Stealing

- ❖ Selling (stolen items)
- ❖ Burglary
- ❖ Murder
- ❖ Gambling
- ❖ Amassing debts

Hence, it has educational, social, cultural, psychological, societal, and governmental facets.[6]

The problem is that no one believes that if there are changes in mental health or personality that it could be considered because of and resulting from drug dependency.

This includes aggressive addiction, which is characterized with a high level of stress in personal relationships and a decline in the level of tolerance as well as a feeling of stress within oneself and self-esteem. If psychological studies were based upon knowledge-based research, then some light would be shed upon the different aspects of the problem. However, it is not possible to categorize narcotics with their various facets.

Drug abuse leads to fundamental change in personality. Hence, it makes the person susceptible to psychological and psychotic illnesses.[7]

---

[6] Source: Al-Jazeerah Website (2001): Drugs are the Scourge of the Era

[7] The definition of psychotic illness is: Psychosis. It is a term used to describe a specific mental illness. Psychosis has a number of illnesses, which most people deem abnormal. They include hallucinations; such as hearing voices when there is no one around; and delusions; such as the person thinking that someone is opposing him or conspiring against him. Some forms of psychosis have bodily causes; such as the brain being afflicted with an illness that results from general paralysis which results from syphilis. And this is a genital illness. Or perhaps the brain can be affected by a natural illness in another part of the body; as is the case in the psychosis due to pneumonia. This is called psychosis of the body. In

THE EFFECTS OF DRUGS

There are serious effects which are customary to (the use of) Hashish. From the most prominent of them:

- ❖ Stress, worry, and paranoia;[8] specifically as it relates to new users.

---

the case of toxic psychosis, a harmful or poisonous substance can affect the brain. From the examples of that is the psychosis that results from lead poisoning. There are other types of psychosis that have no clear bodily cause. The type of psychosis that is the most wide spread is schizophrenia. Refer to The Arabic World Encyclopedia, under: Psychosis.

[8] The definition of paranoia is: In the past, paranoia meant chronic psychosis. This is since the term "paranoia" is derived from the Greek word: Bara, which means aspect, and: Noia which means: mind. So the word, by bringing together its two parts, means: An aspect of the mind and logic. This is psychosis. Psychosis means a type of ill thoughts, which take place, primarily, in connection to the person as it relates to reality and logic. In most cases he is overcome by thoughts which are not logical; the sick person believes in them with firmness and absolute conviction. He does not accept any argument in spite of the fact that none agrees with him. Moreover, it meaning is broad. Symptoms of paranoia: exaggeration in estimation of oneself and an inflated sense of "I"; also, a loss of flexibility in judgment, or that which is called: mental rigidity. So he sees himself to always be correct and that he is upon the truth; and that the people are opposing him; and in many cases the sick person is delusional, thinking he is being followed. In this illness, the sick person blames his problems on other people and he thinks himself to be a victim due to their conspiring against him. In opposition to this, the sick person sees himself at other times to be in a state of pleasure and ease sense of self-satisfaction; and he believes that he is superior and feels an exaggerated sense of vigor. This is what makes these individuals arrogant and egotistical; looking down upon the people and none is able to criticize them. So they are exaggerated in amazement at themselves. In spite of having a good level of intelligence, there is this disorder in judgment, which has an effect upon their emotional life, which leads to turmoil within their societal life. They are always in doubt and very wary. They hate crowds and a lot of companionship. They remain in a wakeful state and are always wary; fearing that there is a conspiracy against them. However, along with this, he deems himself to be living within a nightmare of delusions, and he can do nothing except withdraw and remain secluded. If he is placed in charge, then he is a rigid leader or

- ❖ Cognitive weakness; specifically with regards to focusing and memory.
- ❖ Weakness in psychological faculties.
- ❖ Delayed response in action; from that which results in the risk of road and car accidents. Other dangers also occur due to symptoms of psychosis between these addicts who have a history of psychiatric illnesses within their family history.

As for the long term effects, then they occur as a result of chronic usage of Hashish for a number of years—although there are opinions which hold that this is not affirmed—there are customary symptoms which the inability to stop or cease abusing it bring about. There are also latent problems just as there are acute effects due to cognitive weakness, which affects the attention span and memory. Also, a decrease in the level of performance and skills as well as academic achievement, with adults. (Martin and Hall 1999)[9]

---

he is a vengeful revolutionary. When these characteristics are somewhat mild, then it is possible for them to mesh with societal life although they deem their life difficult. If these attributes are more severe or obvious then they could be afflicted with delirium. The people afflicted with paranoia are in a number of states. From them: harmful maltreatment; recurring delusions; psychotropic delusions brought about by foreign influences; delusions of licentiousness, hallucinations; and in most cases they are mixed with hallucinations of falsehood. The various types of paranoia manifests themselves in categories; from them for example: structured delusions; hallucinations; (also the) paranoia which entails depression and it takes various forms. From them, for example: depression by way of worry; or stress. There is also dangerous and reckless delusions and psychological and personal delusions, etc.

[9] From an article written by Dr. Salaah Abdul-Muta'aal entitled: The Societal, Psychological, and Educational Dimensions of Drug Addiction; on the Al-Jazeerah website 2001: Drugs are the Scourge of the Era

Narcotics are from the greatest obstacles in the growth of the individual and the society, in terms of health, psychologically, financially, and morally.[10]

(When you) reflect upon the psychological effects of drugs[11] you find that they all lead the addict to aggressiveness. They make him susceptible and ready for any type of violent aggression. Similarly they make him, from another perspective, passive in his personality, and easily driven and directed to action which are not possible for an intelligent person to be pleased with, much less one who is religious.

Take, for example, addiction to stimulants. It could perhaps lead the person to a state of schizophrenia or insanity.

Depressants cause the addict to display aggressive tendencies; and in the case of the reduction of the dose, then the addict is afflicted with fear and shivers in the extremities.

Doctors make a connection between opium and behavioral deviations; such as thievery, homosexuality, and prostitution. Alcohol, in general, causes the addict to be more aggressive; particularly towards women and children. It likewise causes him to lose the ability to have good balance and pronunciation.

---

[10] Health Premises for the Royal Order: Health Harms of Drugs pg. 7
[11] From the Al-Jazeerah website: 2001 Archives: Drugs are the Scourge of the Era. At its end, it is mentioned that the sources are:

1. The National Institute on Drugs Abuse; Drug scope-Alcohol-Public Information Material
2. Mawsoo'ah Maqaatil; Societal and Psychological Matters; Studies on Addiction
3. Doctor 'Alaa Kifaafee: The Problems of Drug Addiction; the Psychological Research
4. The Well-known names within the Arab Lands of Some Types of Drugs, transmitted by Doctor Hossam Arafat; published on the website: Islam Online

Similarly, one is not able to perform sexually, and after a time, from addiction, it causes him to enter a state of hallucination accompanied by feelings of depression. Perhaps the state leads him to commit sex crimes without perceiving it. Its danger increases if it is taken along with narcotic substances, such as heroin or along with antidepressants or sedatives.

Qat addiction brings about anxiety, insomnia, and aggressive behavior, disorientation, trances, mental lethargy, mood swings, depression, and weakness in general perception.

Hashish has an effect upon the central nervous system. However, this effect varies from one addict to the other in accordance with his bodily and intellectual strength, in keeping with the natural disposition of the addict and his tendencies. Hence, perhaps the addict could become preoccupied by his imagination and delusions, just as the user with criminal tendencies could be driven to psychotic outbursts and may even be driven to commit acts with violent traits.

From the psychological harms of cocaine are: Violence, nervousness, psychotic behavior, hallucinations, confusion, anxiety, sadness, loss of appetite, mental instability, and the loss of the ties of friendships.[12]

Terrorism, as has been previously defined as: " The "individuals, groups or states" are the fa'il of the verb. Should read: Aggression committed by individuals, groups or states, oppressively against the individual in regards his religion, blood, intellect, wealth, and honor. It comprises (various) categories of striking fear, harm, threats, and murder without right. It is connected to images of looting, terrorizing the pathways, and highway robbery; and every type of violent act or menace, occurring in the pursuance of committing crimes individually or collectively, and intending to

---

[12] Refer to the Newspaper of the Center of Toxicology in Makkah

cause terror amongst the people or terrorizing them by way of harming them or exposing their life, their liberty, their safety, or their (right to) speech, to danger. From its categories is causing harm to the environment or to one of the general or specific faculties or properties; or exposing one of the national or natural resources to danger.

Upon researching the aggressive behavior connected to addiction to intoxicants and that which it entails of violent and sexual crimes, it is found that addiction amongst prison inmates reaches a level of 50% whilst the crimes for which they entered to prison has increased. These are the likes of the crimes of thievery, violence, burglary, and sex crimes.[13]

It is possible that snorting or inhaling for a long period of time causes paleness in the face, fatigue, forgetfulness, lack of ability to think clearly and reasonably, extreme thirst, weight loss, depression, lack of stability, aggressiveness (a feeling of aggression toward others), feelings of delusional happiness, deficiency of blood cells around the spinal cord and it can cause deterioration of the liver and the kidneys.

It has been mentioned regarding some of them that upon ceasing the addiction (they) enter into hallucinatory states and mental instability and aggression, even towards the most dear of the people to him; his mother, his brothers, and his sisters. So one is afflicted with a psychopathic state—which causes him to lose the sense of community and its requirements—and delusions of aggression.

The one who uses cocaine, when he uses increased dosages, this causes for him a state of irritability and easy agitation,

---

[13] Addiction: Its Causes and Characteristics pg. 167

nervousness, aggression, transgression against others, and loss of sound judgment of situations.[14]

Continual abuse causes a person to deteriorate and causes them harm socially. He becomes impulsive, aggressive, and restless and it could drive him to commit crimes to attain money for this expensive drug. Some women are even led into prostitution.

Addiction to drugs makes the person have a weak and hazy personality; meaning hollow in essence; easy to control; susceptible to suggestion; subject to audio and visual hallucinations.

I have no doubt, as it relates to these symptoms that result from drugs: that they come together to give the individual characteristics of aggression towards himself, his family, and the society and (causing) him to have a weakness in familial and personal ties…

I have no doubt, as it relates to this reality, that drugs are from the nearest paths that lead a person to terrorism!

Perhaps the desire to actualize repentance from drugs is a reason for traversing upon the path of terrorism, since the people of falsehood beautify for him acts of terrorism calling them by other than their (actual) name, so he begins murdering the innocent and those with whom there is a treaty (of peace) as an act in which (according to their claim) martyrdom is sought; blowing up the resources of the land and deeming such to be a heroic act; striking fear and causing chaos (deeming it to be) legislative Jihaad.

Perhaps he has repented; however, he wants to affirm that he is truthful in his Tawbah. He wants to cut off, from himself, all paths

---

[14] Addiction has a Treatment pg. 62

that could lead him to his previous state. So he traverses upon this path in order to emphasize his repentance within himself and cut off the path to a relapse.

Perhaps he traverses upon (the path of) extremism in order to stress to the people that he has repented and turned back (to Allaah) so these people use him to carry out that which they want and deceive him. This is the connection between drugs and terrorism. You see it and it has become clear!

From that which has preceded you know one of the reasons for the immoral backgrounds which are found within many of those who delve into terrorism. The Royal Prince Naayif ibn 'Abdul-'Azeez Aali Sa'ood , Minister of Internal Affairs, said in an interview:

> *"Unfortunately, many of them have backgrounds which are immoral. Know, that by way of this extremism or this action, or those who say to them or deceive them (into thinking that) this action shall erase all of their sins; rather, this (extremism) increases them in sin; and it is) more and more evil."*[15]

So the connection between drugs and terrorism is very clear.

---

[15] Ar-Riyadh Newspaper 21/2/1428 H.

THE REASONS FOR TRAVERSING UPON THE PATH OF DRUGS

It is apparent, and Allaah knows best, that the inclinations to traverse upon the path of drugs go back to the following matters:

- ❖ Perhaps the desire to prove oneself is a reason for traversing upon the path of drugs. Perhaps a youth is from the people of dignity and status amongst the youth. So when they are presented to him, he does not want to reject it in order that that would not decrease his status, or (he does so) in order to satisfy his curiosity. This means that the youth, and other than them from those whom it is feared that they will traverse upon this path, should beware of deeming experimentation (with drugs) — which is brought about by curiosity and so called courage — to be light.
- ❖ Evil companionship, which beautifies for him the performance of this affair or compels him towards it, which he does not perceive.
- ❖ Mental disorder
- ❖ Familial problems
- ❖ Societal problems; from poverty, illness, and ignorance along with weakness in religious motivation
- ❖ Fierce attacks from the enemies of the religion and faith against our society in order to drive it to (a state of) weakness and decline.

TREATMENT AND COMBATTING THE PROBLEM

Practical experience affirms approaching terrorism and drugs from a security standpoint alone is not feasible.

As for drugs, its history makes clear that its abuse is an old human practice and many times is connected to the culture of the people, the societies, habits, and customs. Similarly, addiction to drugs, their manufacture, and sale are organized or a network based upon connections, circumstances, supply, and demand. So the treatment of the problem must be done in a systematic fashion focusing on the societies, trade, supply, and demand. Hence, the treatment is by way of the following affairs:

Decreasing the demand for drugs by way of awareness.

Addressing the economical and societal reasons for addiction. In some of the provinces and areas, the life of the people depends upon drugs and it is impossible to eliminate their production except by establishing projects for economic growth in their place.

From that which lures the youth to addiction is:

1. Underestimating experimentation, prompted by curiosity and so-called courage.
2. Breakdown of the family
3. Educational failure
4. Poverty
5. Unemployment
6. Being influenced by one's environment; from friends, one's town, schools, and universities.

Drug dealers utilize economical and legal covering as well as societal activities and politics to protect them from prosecution.

Therefore, the treatment is in need of leadership and political and security-conscious initiatives for the many facets to the problem, which will be able to protect the society from the infiltration of drug gangs into the influential institutions, affecting and preventing them from attempting to launder the drug money.

The centers for treating the addicts within the Arabic and Islamic lands are still deficient in meeting the needs of all of the sick. Similarly, their methods bring about many hindrances and problems. They still are looked at as being a branch of mental health facilities. Treatment takes a long time with substantial costs and most people are not able to afford it, nor are most governments.[16]

Since prevention is better than treatment and *"An ounce of prevention is better than a pound of cure"* (as they say) then we will mention the following matters:

1. The importance of legal and societal awareness of the dangers of drugs
2. The importance of building individuals who have the skills and religious abilities which make him suitable to combat life's problems and treat them without weakness or dejectedness or a defeatist mentality.
3. The necessity of the family, with all of its members, to respond with this awareness, such that they are vigilant in dealing with each member whom it is feared that he is involved with (drugs); ready to respond, by the permission of Allaah, to his falling into it.
   So if the family notices a change in the behavior of the son such that he becomes neglectful in his studies, his food,

---

[16] Source: Al-Jazeerah website, 2001 archives: Drugs are the Scourge of the Era (with additions)

and his clothing; and he is frequently missing from the home, and he has lost that which he used to have from manners and etiquettes and has become poor in terms of his interactions and is frequently introverted and withdrawn, then these are from the primary signs which are befitting for the family to observe. It is upon them as well to take notice of his friends. Has his group of friends changed, or is there a new element therein? It is also upon the family to cooperate with the authorities so that the protection of their son is possible from circles, which they begin to notice around him, seeking to drive him towards this calamity.[17]

4. It is upon the family to spare its members from psychological problems by way of exerting increased efforts to give importance to its members. So it is upon the parents to allow the children the opportunity to have their opinions and thoughts heard, as well as their views and aspirations, their problems and that which they encounter in their lives. They (the parents) should give them a level of respect and consideration as well as encouragement toward that which they see to be from the good affairs. They should also aid them in projects that they consider beneficial. And there is no harm in giving them some help in projects which they (parents) see that he will not be successful in, if the costs are inexpensive, for the purpose of teaching and supporting him. For error is a means to learning that which is correct. If the children miss out on this from within the family, they will search for it outside of the family; such that the likelihood of evil will be increased.

---

[17] Refer to Health Premises of the Divine Order: The Health Harms of Drugs pg. 22

5. Giving consideration to lectures and sermons which clarify and uncover the dangers of drugs and the ploys of the dealers.

As for terrorism, then its remedy and prevention takes place on a number of levels. On the general level, then (it is done by) teaching the people the fundamentals of Al-Islaam—which will protect them from this ideology and erect a protective wall, by the permission of Allaah—in front of the shady campaigns against our society to cause chaos and unrest.

That is by way of removal of the doubts, which they set out to spread in order that this path be actualized for them. Similarly, the ideologies which are imported and that which they bring within their fold of oppositions to the legislation, for they cause corruption without any civility or concealment. For safety is something which cannot be compromised.

The reality is that the fabric of the society is a strong leader. However, prevention is important. So it is a must that lectures are given concentrating on clarifying to the people these legislative affairs; from the obligation of hearing and obeying the ruler, clinging to the Jamaa'ah, the dangers of separation and avoiding the causes of separation and differing. One cannot be silent from exposing the goals of the groups and their leaders and warning against partisanship.

CLOSING

Thanks are due to those who established this convention or conference. I ask Allaah to place their efforts within the scale of their good deeds and to safeguard for us our youth and our Ummah from every evil; and that He, Glorified be He, repel the plot of the enemies of Al-Islaam (and place it) within their throats; and to make their (plot for our) destruction to be their own destruction.

O Allaah, send prayers and peace upon Muhammad, his family, and his companions.

APPENDIX ONE: THE DANGER OF DRUGS
Shaykh 'Alee Al-Haddaadee[18]

Indeed all the praise is for Allaah. We praise him, we seek his aid, we seek His forgiveness. We seek refuge with Allaah from the evil of our souls and the consequences of our evil actions. He whom Allaah guides there is none to misguide and he whom Allaah leads astray there in none to guide him aright. I bear witness that none has the right to be worshipped except Allaah; who is one without partners; and I bear witness that our Prophet Muhammad is Allaah's servant and Messenger.

O Allaah, send prayers, peace, and blessings upon Your slave and Messenger Muhammad; upon his family, and companions, altogether. As to proceed:

Have Taqwaa of Allaah, as Taqwaa should be had of Him. How great is the reward of those who have Taqwaa. How delightful is the state and the abode of those who are obedient. O people, indeed the punishment for crimes and sins within the Dunyaa and the Hereafter is due to the despicable nature of the crime and its evil effect upon the one who commits it and upon the society. Allaah, the Mighty and Majestic, has said:

﴿ ٱلَّذِينَ كَفَرُوا۟ وَصَدُّوا۟ عَن سَبِيلِ ٱللَّهِ زِدْنَٰهُمْ عَذَابًا فَوْقَ ٱلْعَذَابِ بِمَا كَانُوا۟ يُفْسِدُونَ ﴾ (٨٨)

---

[18] This is from sermon which the Shaykh gave, and the audio can be found on the Shaykh's website: http://www.haddady.com/soundsubject/2.html

Those who disbelieved and hinder (men) from the Path of Allaah, for them We will add torment over the torment; because they used to spread corruption. [19]

Allaah, the Glorified, has said:

$$﴿ وَلَا تُفْسِدُوا۟ فِى ٱلْأَرْضِ بَعْدَ إِصْلَٰحِهَا ۚ ذَٰلِكُمْ خَيْرٌ لَّكُمْ إِن كُنتُم مُّؤْمِنِينَ ۝ ﴾$$

"And do not mischief on the earth after it has been set in order. That will be better for you, if you are believers." [20]

And indeed from the great crimes and the major destructive (sins) and the sins which are destructive to the individual and the society are (the use of) drugs and intoxicants. They do not enter into a society except that they destroy it. No one becomes addicted to them except that he becomes corrupted with various types of destruction. They do not spread within a society except that it is engulfed with every evil and it falls into various types of calamities and major sins occur therein and corruptions occur therein which the intellectuals and righteous are unable to remedy.

'Uthmaan, may Allaah be pleased with him, said:

"Avoid Khamr for it is the mother of (all) evils."[21]

Drugs, O brothers, are the greatest form of Khamr. Therefore, they have been prohibited with the most intense form of prohibition. The types of drugs and their corruptions are many. From them are

---

[19] Soorah An-Nahl (16:88)
[20] Soorah Al-A'raf (7:85)
[21] Reported within Sunan ibn Maajah and graded Saheeh by Shaykh Al-Albaanee

DRUGS AND THEIR EFFECT ON THE MIND
SHAYKH MUHAMMAD BAAZMOOL

those which the people know and from them are those which are not known at all. Drugs, in all of its types, have been prohibited by Allaah and his Messenger (sallallaahu alayhi wa sallam); whether they be plants, pills, eaten, or drank, or snorted, or injected.

Similarly, drugs, in all of its types, the Legislation is sever in its condemnation and threat against it due to what it contains from harm and destruction. And due to that which they contain from evil and due to that which they cause for the addict, from transforming him to an evil person from whom corruption and crime are expected and no good is hoped for from him.

The intellectuals of the world have called for the saving of the societies from the scourge of drugs due to that which they have witnessed from iniquities.

The harms of drugs upon the one addicted to them and upon the society are many and nearly none are safe except a small portion. From their harms upon the addict is the loss of his intellect; and the intellect is the distinguishing characteristic between the human and the animals. He whose intellect goes then he embarks upon crimes and his virtue is taken from him.

From their harms is that the natural disposition of the person changes and he becomes a Shaytaan and he is stripped of the characteristics of the righteous.

From their harms is foolishness in manner of dealings. So he does that which is harmful to him and abandons that which benefits him. Shaytaan has driven him to every despicable act and has removed him from every virtue.

From the harms of drugs is corruption in the thought process. So he loses sound judgment and upright opinions. He does not see the end results of the affairs and he does not look except to the exact moment that he is currently in, even if it contains his destruction, harm, and detriment.

From their harms is the loss of trustworthiness and negligence regarding it in that which is obligatory to safeguard and preserve. He cannot be trusted over any general thing; nor can he be trusted over wealth or job. He can't even be trusted over his relatives and family members. This is because the drugs have corrupted his nature, and the refuge is with Allaah.

From its harms is that the addict is a burden upon the society. He does not bring any good to his society nor is he successful in that which he brings forth.

From its harms is that the addict is despised and hated, even by the closest of people to him.

From its harms is the squandering of wealth and the inability to make noble earnings. So he resorts to earning wealth by way of criminal means. I seek Allaah's refuge for me and for you.

From its harms is deterioration of one's health and the contraction of incurable diseases, leading the person to death.

From its harms is the loss of dignity and inclining towards the wicked, from men or women.

From its harms is the shortening of life due to what it causes from destruction of the bodily organs and due to what is exposes the person to from grief and stress.

From its harms is the Shayateen gaining mastery over the addict and the angels of mercy being far away from him, until he is driven to the Hellfire, and the refuge is with Allaah. Allaah, the Mighty and Majestic said:

﴿ وَمَن يَعْشُ عَن ذِكْرِ ٱلرَّحْمَٰنِ نُقَيِّضْ لَهُۥ شَيْطَٰنًا فَهُوَ لَهُۥ قَرِينٌ ۝ وَإِنَّهُمْ لَيَصُدُّونَهُمْ عَنِ ٱلسَّبِيلِ وَيَحْسَبُونَ أَنَّهُم مُّهْتَدُونَ ۝ حَتَّىٰٓ إِذَا جَآءَنَا قَالَ يَٰلَيْتَ بَيْنِي وَبَيْنَكَ بُعْدَ ٱلْمَشْرِقَيْنِ فَبِئْسَ ٱلْقَرِينُ ۝ وَلَن يَنفَعَكُمُ ٱلْيَوْمَ إِذ ظَّلَمْتُمْ أَنَّكُمْ فِي ٱلْعَذَابِ مُشْتَرِكُونَ ۝ ﴾

"And whosoever turns away (blinds himself) from the remembrance of the Most Beneficent (Allaah) (i.e. this Qur'aan and worship of Allaah), We appoint for him Shaytaan (Satan devil) to be a Qarîn (an intimate companion) to him. And verily, they (devils) hinder them from the Path (of Allaah), but they think that they are guided aright! Till, when (such a one) comes to Us, he says [to his Qarîn (Satan / devil companion)] "Would that between me and you were the distance of the two easts (or the east and west)" a worst (type of) companion (indeed)! It will profit you not this Day (O you who turn away from Allaah's remembrance and His worship, etc.) as you did wrong, (and) that you will be sharers (you and your Qarîn) in the punishment." [22]

From its harms is the curse being upon the addict until he repents. This is due to his (sallallaahu alayhi wa sallam) statement:

لَعَنَ اللهُ الْخَمْرَ وَ شَارِبَهَا وَ سَاقِيهَا وَ مُبْتَاعَهَا وَ بَائِعَهَا وَ عَاصِرَهَا وَ مُعْتَصِرَهَا وَ حَامِلَهَا وَ الْمَحْمُولَةَ إِلَيْهِ .

---

[22] Soorah Az-Zukhruf (43:36-39)

"Allaah has cursed Al-Khamr; the one who drinks it and the one who pours it; its buyer and its seller; its squeezer and the one for whom it is squeezed; the one who carries it and the one to whom it is carried."[23]

And he (sallallaahu alayhi wa sallam) said:

ثَلَاثَةٌ لَا يَدْخُلُونَ الْجَنَّةَ مدمن الْخَمرِ وَ عَابِدُ الْوَثَنِ وَ الدِيوث

"Three will not enter into Paradise: The one who is addicted to intoxicants; the worshipper of the idol; and the pimp."[24]

Drugs, O brothers, is greater than Khamr (alcohol). Therefore, the prohibition of Khamr is a prohibition of drugs as well; and the threat regarding alcohol is likewise a threat regarding drugs.

From its harms, O brothers in faith, is the spread of various types of crime within the society and the spread of lewdness and evils; and the loss of the family structure, and the deviation of the

---

[23] Reported within Al-Jaami As-Sagheer; Al-Albaanee graded it as Saheeh

[24] Translator's note: I was not able to find the version of the Hadeeth mentioned by the Shaykh. However, from the versions I found was one with the wording:

ثلاثة لا يدخلون الجنة العاق لوالديه ومدمن الخمر والمنان بما أعطى

"Three will not enter into Paradise: The one who is disrespectful towards his parents; the one who is addicted to intoxicants; and the one who reminds others of what he has given."

Reported within As-Silsilah As-Saheehah no. 674 graded Hasan by Al-Albaanee.

younger generation; for they will live without a family or cultivator for them to find repose with.

From the harms of drugs upon the society is the descending of punishments and tribulations. Allaah, the Mighty and Majestic, said:

$$﴿ وَٱتَّقُوا۟ فِتْنَةً لَّا تُصِيبَنَّ ٱلَّذِينَ ظَلَمُوا۟ مِنكُمْ خَآصَّةً ۖ وَٱعْلَمُوٓا۟ أَنَّ ٱللَّهَ شَدِيدُ ٱلْعِقَابِ ﴿٢٥﴾ ﴾$$

And fear the Fitnah (affliction and trial, etc.) which affects not in particular (only) those of you who do wrong (but it may afflict all the good and the bad people), and know that Allaah is Severe in punishment. [25]

From its harms is obedience will come to be a burden; it will be disliked, and hated. Likewise, dislike and hatred for the righteous, and avoiding their gatherings and staying away from the gatherings of remembrance and the places of worship; and love for crime and inclination towards disobedience; and love for the evil people; taking them and friends and companions.

Brothers in Islaam, drugs; the devils of mankind grow them, manufacture, and distribute them in order to actualize the objectives which they have:

The First Objective: To corrupt the society to the point that the one who is addicted to drugs does not think except in ways which are blameworthy (even) by the animals. When it spreads within the society and it is not combatted, then (others) will be harmed by it and by way of it be destroyed.

---

[25] Soorah Al-Anfal (8:25)

The Second Objective: To earn Haraam monies; and what an evil earning this is. Money that is acquired by way of drugs and intoxicants contains no good nor is there any blessing in it. Rather, it corrupts the heart and ruins the homes and disperses the families and destroys them. It brings about disgrace, shame, and the cutting off of the lineage.

O Muslims, beware of the traps of Shaytaan with which he traps his followers in order that they will be with him in the Hellfire.

APPENDIX TWO: DRUG MONEY FROM BEFORE ISLAAM
Shaykh 'Abdul-Qaadir Al-Junayd[26]

Question:

A man used to sell drugs before Islaam, then he became Muslim. Now, he has a lot of money from that time. He asks, what is upon him as it relates to this money? Is it permissible for him to give charity and make Hajj from it?

Answer:

This money belongs to him; because Islaam wipes away that which came before it; clear? Al-Islaam wipes away that which came before it. The Prophet, when the disbelievers of the Quraysh would embrace Al-Islaam, no doubt they had many impermissible dealings; clear? Yet he did not command them to get rid of their wealth which was derived from Haraam.

---

[26] This question was asked to the Shaykh on 3 Rajab 1433/ May 25, 2012

APPENDIX THREE: DRUG MONEY FROM AFTER ISLAAM
Shaykh Abdul-Qaadir Al-Junayd[27]

Question: Shaykh, I asked you before about a man who used to sell drugs then accepted Islaam, and what was due upon him as it relates to the money from that time; and you responded to me. However, the questioner informed me that his intention was not that the man was a disbeliever. Rather, he was a Muslim who sold drugs then repented. So what is due upon him as it relates to his money?

Answer: The drug money that is with him, it is not permissible for him to take anything from it. Rather, he is to spend it in in the welfare of the community and the paths of good. Clear? The money which the Muslim acquires through impermissible means, it is not permissible for him to consume it (i.e., to benefit himself with it). If it belongs to a certain people, then it is obligatory that he return it to them (i.e. he stole it or robbed them). If it doesn't belong to anyone, then he spends it in the welfare of the community and he does not eat from it, nor does he feed his family with it.

---

[27] This question was asked approximately one month after the previous question mentioned in appendix two.